Alfred Gurney

A ramble through the United States

a lecture delivered in S. Barnabas' School, February 3, 1886

Alfred Gurney

A ramble through the United States
a lecture delivered in S. Barnabas' School, February 3, 1886

ISBN/EAN: 9783744740883

Printed in Europe, USA, Canada, Australia, Japan

Cover: Foto ©ninafisch / pixelio.de

More available books at **www.hansebooks.com**

A RAMBLE

THROUGH

THE UNITED STATES

A LECTURE

DELIVERED (IN PART) IN S. BARNABAS' SCHOOL

FEBRUARY 3, 1886.

BY

ALFRED GURNEY, M.A.

VICAR OF S. BARNABAS', PIMLICO

AUTHOR OF "THE VISION OF THE EUCHARIST," "A CHRISTMAS FAGGOT"

[*NOT PUBLISHED*]

TO

CYRIL,

WITH A FATHER'S LOVE,

AND TO THE OTHER COMPANIONS OF MY HOLIDAY,

ARTHUR HENRY STANTON

AND

CYRIL EDWARDS,

THESE PAGES ARE INSCRIBED

PREFACE.

This brief account of a parson's holiday is an attempt to fulfil a promise to my people of a lecture on America. It is not published, the ground traversed and the scenes and places described being already familiar enough to those who visit, or who read books about, the United States. It has rather outgrown, in the course of writing, the limits of a lecture, as the desire grew upon me to retain and deepen the many impressions made by a first visit to the New World. I am printing it that my hearers may have, if they like, the opportunity of reading what in the lecture-room I was obliged to omit; and also that I may have the pleasure of placing it in the hands of a few of my friends on both sides of the Atlantic, to whom I am indebted for many kindnesses.

A RAMBLE THROUGH THE UNITED STATES.

So familiar to most people nowadays is the voyage across the Atlantic, that little need be said about the first stage of our westward travels. Every one knows that the three thousand miles, which it took Columbus three months to traverse, are now crossed with ease in little more than a week. By the fastest of the Cunard liners it has been done in less. And yet the man must be singularly wanting in imagination who can find himself for the first time on the deck of an Atlantic steamer, with his back towards the Old World, and his face towards the New, and remain unmoved. My travels in Europe, Asia, and Africa had brought me face to face with the beauties of many an enchanted land whose magic spell was of the Past. The traveller in America finds his imagination exercised by a counter-charm that constrains him to speculate about the Future. The concluding stanza of one of Lowell's finest poems utters a truth, to the full meaning of which I have only gradually awakened with the gathered experience of years, and it is perhaps the truth that American travel chiefly enforces—

> "New occasions teach new duties; Time makes ancient good uncouth;
> They must upward still, and onward, who would keep abreast of Truth;
> Lo, before us gleam her camp-fires! we ourselves must Pilgrims be,
> Launch our *Mayflower*, and steer boldly through the desperate winter sea,
> Nor attempt the Future's portal with the Past's blood-rusted key."

But, apart from such considerations, the sea itself is a wonder ever new, and to any child of nature the lovely commerce of winds and waters opens fountains of joy not easily exhausted. Our voyage was not altogether uneventful; we encountered something of a storm at starting, which put landing at Queenstown out of the question; the usual cold fog off the sandbanks of Newfoundland on the fifth day from Liverpool; and, to conclude with, an exquisite Sunday of unclouded sunshine. As the stars came out one by one, bright-eyed watchers in the solemn death-chamber of the departed sun, we dropped anchor within the bar of New York harbour. I must not omit to record, as they were the most delightful experiences of the whole voyage, two of the loveliest sunsets I ever saw at sea. Sea sunsets are not more beautiful than sunsets on land, but they have their own special and unspeakable charm; and to most of us the sea sunsets of a lifetime are few in number, and, coming at long intervals, they are the more memorable. It is surely a significant parable of Nature that with the death of the sun comes the day's transfiguration. The broad expanse of waters and the unbroken horizon furnish a fitting stage for the glorious pageant. As he swoons and sinks, and at length falls, death-stricken, in loveliest disarray on his soft couch, the spirit of Beauty seems to arise and spread her rosy wings, with a promise of resurrection in the rapture of her far-seeing eyes and palpitating breast, as she broods over the watery sepulchre of his unquenched, though vanished, majesty. It would be difficult even in Tennyson to find two more exquisite stanzas than the following, in which, with an accuracy to which only poets may aspire, he describes sunset and moonlight at sea—

> "How oft we saw the sun retire,
>   And burn the threshold of the night,
> Fall from his ocean-lane of fire,
>   And sleep beneath his pillared light!
> How oft the purple-skirted robe
>   Of twilight slowly downward drawn,
> As thro' the slumber of the globe
>   Again we dashed into the dawn!

> "New stars all night above the brim
>   Of waters lightened into view;
> They climbed as quickly, for the rim
>   Changed every moment as we flew.
> Far ran the naked moon across
>   The houseless ocean's heaving field,
> Or flying shone the silver boss
>   Of her own halo's dusky shield."

One other event of the voyage let me record, since I am seeking to recall emotions. We had a death on board. It occurred among the steerage passengers, a man who was travelling alone, and of whom nothing was known except that he had been of intemperate habits. We saw his body consigned to the keeping of the great waters which lie in the hollow of God's hand, against the day when the sea shall give up her dead. The simple ritual was performed with impressive solemnity in the midst of a silent and awe-stricken crowd—many of them emigrants; and the officiating priest, a Roman Catholic, spoke a few earnest words to those who stood around.

The following verses, composed on board the *Aurania*, will, I think, best express the thoughts suggested by the voyage; and, still pausing on the threshold of my difficult task—the attempt to share with you my impressions of the United States—let me read them, as we are preparing to plant our feet for the first time on the shores of the New World.

FOOTPRINTS ON THE ATLANTIC.

Footprints on the broad Atlantic
   Let us reverently trace;
Pilgrim-footsteps moving westward,
   Men of every creed and race,
Seeking, till the restless waters
   Yield a resting-place.

Westward moves the great procession,
    Westward still, whate'er befall;
So the father of the faithful
    Shaped his course, for God did call;
Westward rode the Magi, westward
    Swelled the sails of Paul.

Through long years men questioned, wondered,
    (Hope must doubt and fear outrun),
Hide the western waves a treasure
    Buried 'neath the setting sun?
Came at length the great Adventure,
    And the prize was won!

By a phantom fleet encompassed,
    Steer we for the fabled West;
From the foremost prow Columbus,
    Hope-enkindled, faith-possest,
Points us forward, self-devoted
    To a sacred quest.*

Steal across the sea at sundown
    Fragments of a sacred song;
'Tis the vesper hymn to Mary,
    Heard the winds and waves among,
Sung by Spanish sailors; sea nymphs
    Still the strain prolong.

England's heroes quickly follow,
    And the English flag is seen
Traversing the stormy waters
    Which 'twixt two worlds intervene,
Claiming the discovered country
    For her virgin-queen.

---

* "He seemed too much absorbed by the great cause to which he had consecrated his life, to allow scope for the lower pursuits and pleasures which engage ordinary men."—PRESCOTT.

> In their wake another vessel
>   Sails, a blossom on the wave; *
> Exiles are the hearts that man her,
>   Pilgrim-fathers, stern and brave,
> Making for a land of freedom,
>   Or a salt sea grave.
>
> Voices raised in loud defiance,
>   On Atlantic breezes borne,
> Tell of strife; the quarrel ended,
>   Breaks at length a brighter morn;
> Child and mother face each other,
>   Love subduing scorn.
>
> Footprints on the broad Atlantic,
>   Be it yours and mine to trace;
> Westward still the great procession
>   Travels; one in creed and race,
> May America and England
>   Evermore embrace!

One little incident of our landing may be noticed as illustrating at once the friendliness and the smartness which are such familiar characteristics of the American people. We were awaiting the visitation of the Custom House officer, when a gentleman, whom we had met on the boat, came forward, and most kindly offered his services in order to facilitate our passage through the Custom House. He at once addressed himself to the officer, and assured him that we were English clergymen, and had nothing to declare—"no baggage at all," he proceeded, observing us with a discriminating eye,

---

* The ship in which the Pilgrim Fathers sailed was called the *Mayflower*.

"except, I suppose, their shaving apparatus and their vestments!"

After a day at New York spent in necessary preparations, including a visit to the Sisters of S. John Baptist's House (Clewer) for the purpose of borrowing some altar-linen, we started by the Hudson River boat for Albany and Saratoga. A European may be permitted to demur, but Mr. Curtis is at least not open to the charge of extravagance when, comparing the Hudson with the most famous rivers of Europe, he says, "The Danube has in part glimpses of such grandeur, the Elbe has sometimes such delicately pencilled effects, but no European river is so lordly in its bearing, none flows in such state to the sea." The Palisades (as the cliffs are called), the Highlands, and the Catskill mountains are all of them beautiful features, that would make the reputation of any river, and there are many beautiful houses and villas, and many a thriving town on the sloping banks. But the ice-houses are a peculiar feature that deserves a passing notice. They are enormous sheds, without either doors or windows, and carefully packed from top to bottom with ice, the harvest of the winter months, for the use of New York, whose annual consumption of ice is upwards of seven hundred thousand tons. There are nearly two hundred of these ice-houses on the river bank. "The use of ice in America," writes Mr. Pidgeon, "is carried to an extent totally unknown in other countries, no matter how hot their summers, and the business of ice-collecting is conducted on a correspondingly gigantic scale. The total annual ice-crop of the States is estimated at twenty million tons, of which the Hudson alone furnishes about three million tons, a quantity that could neither be gathered, stored, nor distributed without the assistance of special apparatus."

We landed at Albany, the capital of New York State. It was settled originally by the Dutch as early as 1614, and in 1664 was named in honour of the Duke of York and Albany, afterwards James II. The Dutch taste for excessive cleanliness within doors seems long to have survived. A traveller, who visited Albany in 1776, gives the following amusing description, preserved by McMaster in his admirable history of the "People of the United States": "I was not a little surprised to find Albany to be so dirty a city, the houses in the Dutch taste, the insides clean to a fault; even their cyder barrels are kept scoured as clean as their dishes; their women are continually employed in scouring the floors; one drop of ink in a house will breed a riot, till it is erased by soap and sand and dishclouts."

Taking the train at Albany, we reached Saratoga Springs by nightfall. This renowned and much frequented watering-place possesses twenty-eight springs, all largely charged with carbonic acid gas. The hotels here are the largest in the world. There are two with over a thousand rooms, and accommodation for nearly twice that number of guests. Here we made our first acquaintance with a "buggy," lightest and most commodious of small vehicles, and drove to the Saratoga Lake over the broadest and smoothest of roads, favourable to the fast trotting in which Americans delight, and in which their horses excel, the mile having been done in less than two minutes and a quarter. We saw some very good performances. The lake was reached just at the right time, when most of the pleasure-seekers had gone home, turning their backs on the sunset-glow which was flushing sky and water, and making of the world an enchanted place. It was the first of many similar splendours of the evening skies which day after day our eyes were permitted to feast upon, and which, had our path lain through swamps and deserts, would have sufficed to make it glorious and memorable, so manifold and exquisite were the combinations, gradations, and pulsations of many-coloured light.

A rapid night journey brought us from Saratoga Springs to Niagara Falls. Of Niagara I shall attempt no description. The attempt has often been made, but never with success; no pen, no brush is equal to such a task. Two things only let me mention which have not perhaps been sufficiently noticed ; (1) the exceeding loveliness of its surroundings, and (2) the movement of waters rising as well as falling. The trees on its wooded banks, under the constant benediction of its ceaseless spray, are surpassingly green, fresh and rich in foliage, giving an adorned, Eden-like appearance to the whole landscape, which adds greatly to its beauty. Niagara is in truth, a waterfall in a garden. And the abundant waters, the purest surely in the world, which dance and sing and leap and shout, and at length plunge in thunder over the abyss, send up such a towering cloud of scattering spray, that it gives the impression of a transparent veil being ever lifted by invisible hands for the fuller disclosure of the majestic loveliness behind, which, like all created beauty, speaks of a Beauty uncreated, and of the self-concealment by which alone it can reveal itself to human eyes. Here, more than elsewhere, the loveliness of Nature shows like a stately ritual that expresses and enshrines an Invisible Presence, of which it is the appropriate drapery. The ultimate charm, the divine secret of Niagara, no less than of the tiniest flower, is only to be discovered by the intervention of a spiritual agency nearer to us than anything that our eyes look upon, the anointed and anointing Word, by whose unction only can we know or see anything aright.

Leaving Niagara for a day, with the intention of returning for a last look, we crossed Lake Ontario to Toronto, after Montreal the largest city in Canada, and a place of growing importance. In comparison with the States, Canada is no doubt poor, not in natural beauty, but in interest. An Englishman, however, cannot forget the loyal and unshaken attachment to the British throne which has all along characterized the Dominion, ever since, on the heights of Abraham above Quebec, the victory of Wolfe crushed for ever the power of France in the Western Continent. Returning by rail, we spent the night at Hamilton, where we encountered a magnificent thunder-storm, and got back to Cataract House in time for breakfast.

I would recommend every one at Niagara who wishes to taste the sweetness of a new sensation, to brave the imaginary dangers of the Cave of the Winds, put on the bathing-dress, and descend into the centre of the water-world by the steps and bridges that have been skilfully constructed underneath the American Fall. You find yourself stepping in and out of circular rainbows (bows no longer) which form and fade and re-form above, around, beneath you; and you can finish up with such a shower-bath as I never imagined. For one brief moment the ecstasy of a water-spirit, at rest and at play in the heart of Niagara, may be yours.

We were fortunate in having two last views of the world's wonder; the first from Luna Island above the American Fall; and the second—a surprise— from the railway where it skirts the rapids above the Horse-shoe Fall. Oh, those diverging and converging streams; those careering rapids; that racing, bending river; that circling whirlpool; that encompassing loveliness of ever fresh greenery; that tremulous cloud of ever-ascending spray; and the sustained and solemn thunder of those plunging waters! To have seen Niagara is a life-long possession.

The journey from Niagara to Colorado Springs, broken only for a few hours at Chicago, was somewhat tedious; and owing to a violent rain-storm, which destroyed the road both before and behind us, and obliged us to wait a whole day at a wayside station, we reached our destination just twenty-four hours behind time. This is apparently no uncommon occurrence. The exquisite beauty of Manitou, however, five miles nearer the mountains on the Pike's Peak trail, to which we hurried on, and where we were welcomed by the kindest of friends, made ample compensation for the fatigue of the journey and the monotony of the prairies.

> "Beneath the rocky peak that hides
> In clouds its snow-flecked crest,
> Within those crimson crags, abides
> An Orient in the West."

It was a delight not to be easily described to find ourselves embowered in a garden, green and flowery, secluded and homelike, as any lovely nook in old England itself, with a mountain stream singing its perpetual song on one side of the velvet lawn, and overshadowed by the magnificent Peak. Visitors to Manitou know well the beauty of Briarhurst, and the hospitality of Dr. and Mrs. Bell.

Reserving Colorado Springs for the return journey, we commenced the passage of the great mountain chain, towards which we had been gradually ascending for some hundreds of miles by a romantic line of railway, a masterpiece of engineering skill, leading over the La Veta Pass and the Toltec Gorge and climbing to a height of 9486 feet. We reached, after a delightful journey of twenty hours, Durango, the centre of the San Juan mining district, where by the light of a full moon we visited a silver mine. Continuing the journey next day, we mounted to the roof of the cars, and enjoyed an ascent of extraordinary beauty, which brought us to Silverton, another mining town in the very heart of a mountainous region, the magnificence of which it would be difficult to exaggerate. Here, under the best of guidance, we had an opportunity of still further improving our acquaintance with the miners and their underground operations. It was interesting in the bowels of the earth to discern, like a faint smile on a slumbering face, the dim lustre and colour of the precious metals. "The silver is Mine, and the gold is Mine, saith the Lord of Hosts:" a truth of which others need to be reminded as much perhaps as miners. The following day was one of the most memorable of the whole journey. We struck across the mountains on horseback, and a ride of twenty miles—one of the loveliest I have ever taken—brought us across the "continental divide" (watershed), and under the shadow of the Red Mountain, descending by a glorious canyon to Ouray, a village that bears the name of an illustrious Indian chief. Though at so great a height—the summit of the pass is over eleven thousand feet—it will live in my memory as the most flowery path of all that it was my fortune to tread in the Western Continent. Then came a drive of forty miles, and we struck soon after nightfall the railway at Montrose. Here we took the train for Salt Lake City, and, traversing a desert flanked for many miles by remarkable sandhills that had the appearance of carefully constructed fortifications, reached, after sixteen hours in the cars, the head-quarters of the Latter Day Saints. The carriage in which we drove to the hotel was drawn by four milk-white horses of high breeding, worthy of a royal wedding. Was it a sign? and, if so, what the signification?

The industry and enterprise of this strange people have turned a wilderness into a garden. The bee-hive, emblem of industrious toil, is one of their favourite symbols. They came from a far country under the leadership of Joseph Smith, the founder of the sect; a man who, if he had nothing else to recommend him, must certainly have possessed some capacity and much audacity. It would seem that he was an impostor rather than a fanatic, with a marvellous gift of arousing and trading on the fanaticism of others. In 1844 Smith had the hardihood to offer himself as a candidate for the Presidency of the United States; but in the course of the same year his career was cut short by a violent death.

Brigham Young was his successor, a man of undeniable ability, despotic and unscrupulous; and by him a multitude of people, to some extent disciplined and ennobled by the hardships they overcame and the persecution they endured, were led into their land of promise, and the settlement at Salt Lake City was established. A river, named after the Jordan, which finds its grave in the Salt Lake at some distance from the city, supplied water for the irrigation that was alone necessary to fertilize the sandy soil, and the result is one of the most beautiful cities in the world, with a population of twenty-two thousand souls, including some eight thousand "Gentiles," as those who are not Mormons are significantly called. Two monster buildings disfigure the place, the tabernacle and temple, probably the ugliest erections in the world. The latter is a massive and lofty stone structure, and when finished will contain various chambers for the performance of the Mormon marriages and other ritual services. The former is the place of assembly on Sundays for the whole Mormon community, and is a huge building, oval in shape and quite unadorned, capable of seating many thousands, and possessed of acoustic properties that are quite extraordinary. Its only treasure is an organ, one of the largest in the States, which had been lately made to yield, we were amused to hear, very unaccustomed strains, suggestive of the Savoy Theatre, under the skilful hands of Sir Arthur Sullivan himself.

Anxious to learn something about Mormonism from within, and not rest content with hostile criticism, I had obtained in England a letter of introduction to one of the so-called apostles, and it was a disappointment to find on my arrival in Salt Lake City that he had quite recently died. The Book of Mormon is, however, its own refutation and condemnation, and all that I was able to learn about the principles and practices of the sect in America confirmed the unfavourable impression. Polygamy, or, as it is officially called, "plurality," was no part of the original revelation, but a later development, not authorized till the "Celestial Law of Marriage" was published in 1852. Charles Kingsley, when he visited Salt Lake City, refused even to enter the tabernacle and temple, so sensible was he of the scandal of a system, claiming to be religious, that deliberately degrades womanhood, and corrupts and subverts family life. The women at Salt Lake City looked like slaves, ugly and miserable. But the place has a lovely situation and aspect; the trim gardens are adorned with the fairest of flowers and the most fruitful of fruit trees; the fertilizing streams run pleasantly under shadow of the trees that flank the broad streets; and every one seems thriving and prosperous. It is difficult to believe that the presence of troops in the neighbouring Fort Douglas, where a permanent camp has been established, alone keeps the peace, and prevents the lives of those who reject the Mormon yoke from being sacrificed to the fanatical frenzy of the "saints." There are very few Americans among them; they are chiefly recruited from Norway, Denmark, England, and Scotland, Wales sending a large contingent. It was in 1830 that the sect was started, and ten years ago they were said to number two hundred and fifty thousand, eighty thousand of whom live in the territory of Utah, and the rest scattered through the world. Most of them have belonged to some Protestant sect, and with hardly an exception they are grossly ignorant. The system is one of the most high-handed spiritual tyranny, the creation of unscrupulous and profligate men; but in the ranks are to be found, no doubt, many earnest and simple souls, who have not detected the delusion to which they have fallen victims. A determined effort is at length being made by the Government of the United States to enforce the law against bigamy, and it is to be hoped that without undue severity a monster-scandal may be suppressed.

Leaving Salt Lake City, we travelled for a day and a night due north, and at Beaver Canyon left the railroad, and made for Yellow Stone Park across the prairies, a drive of a hundred miles, in a stage waggon and four horses. Game was plentiful, and an occasional shot from the box-seat did execution enough to set our minds at rest as to the sufficiency and quality of our supper. The night was passed in a romantic spot on the Snake River, where we slept for the first time under canvas. The following afternoon we entered the Park, and found rough quarters at a place bearing the expressive name of Fire Hole Bason. Yellow Stone Park, the wonderland of America, is situated partly in the territory of Wyoming, partly in that of Montana. It is sixty-five miles north and south by fifty-five east and west in extent, and no part of it is less than six thousand feet above the sea level. It is a grand mountainous region, clothed with vast forests, and containing some hundreds of geysers and some thousands of hot springs, many of them literally boiling. It suggests a world on fire, but a fire that is the cherisher, not the destroyer, of life. We were, unfortunately, a day too late to see the "Bee Hive" geyser, one of the finest, in a state of eruption; but "Old Faithful," so called from the regularity of its action, performed three times for our benefit, and a strangely beautiful sight it was. Some of these crystal fountains send their diamond spray to a height of two hundred feet. They suggest a gigantic subterranean caldron—if so homely an illustration be permissible—continually boiling over. We encountered a severe thunder-storm before which we raced home for shelter; and next day, on reaching the Yellow Stone River and Canyon, we found that the neighbouring lake had been the scene of a sad tragedy. A boat containing four men had been struck by lightning; one had been killed on the spot, and the others made insensible. All would have lost their lives had not the boat, which was fortunately near the shore, drifted in, for the electric current had made a hole in the bottom. The dead man was a solitary traveller, and as no one knew his home or his friends, he was buried beside the lake.

No words can describe the beauty of the Yellow Stone Canyon. The river makes two magnificent leaps, the upper and the lower falls, and on each side the cliffs rise to the height of a thousand feet. But the special and pre-eminent charm of the place is its colour, caused by the various deposits. We made our way on horseback through the woods that crown the ravine, and gazed down on a scene quite unlike anything I had ever looked upon before, and one which I can never forget. All loveliest colours seemed to be blended on those mighty walls, sculptured by the joint action of fire and water, orange, purple, crimson, and primrose being the predominant hues. They seemed to glow responsive to the rapture of the sunset, earth for once almost eclipsing the beauty of the sky. The angels of Fra Angelico might have winged their way from Florence, and sentinelled those cliffs, or passed in glad procession up and down that canyon, without in any way disturbing, with their radiant faces and brilliant robes, the harmony of colour. Two eagle's nests we observed built on the summit of rocky pinnacles far below us, and the mother birds, sailing round and bringing up fish for their young ones, lent a touch of family life to the enchanting scene.

We left Yellow Stone Park on the north by the

Mammoth Hot Springs on the slope of the White Mountain, passing from Wyoming into Montana, and at Cinnabar struck the Northern Pacific Railway. Another thousand miles of rapid travelling to the inspiring cry of "Westward Ho!" and we shall be on the Pacific coast. The journey occupied three days, the last day, unfortunately a wet one, being spent on the magnificent Columbia River, whose salmon fisheries feed the markets of the world.

Throughout this wild north-western region big game is plentiful. The only bears we encountered were in a state of captivity, tethered to poles at the hotels and railway stations, but we occasionally came upon the track of a bear, and we had the satisfaction of tasting a bear-steak. The grizzly bear, of which we heard stories from the hunters, is a very ugly customer, large as a polar bear, very fierce, and difficult to kill, his head being nearly bullet-proof. Panthers too, in these parts commonly called "mountain-lions," are to be met with;* elks also, and occasionally buffaloes, though they have become of late years extremely scarce. Formerly huge herds used to roam the country, and stop the trains sometimes for hours. We came across antelopes

* "The names of many animals in the New World have been frequently borrowed from the Old: but the species are very different."—PRESCOTT.

"When the Spaniards landed in America, they did not find a single animal they were acquainted with: not one of the quadrupeds of Europe, Asia, or Africa."—LAWRENCE.

more than once; and on the rivers beautiful waterfowl. The prairie dogs are curious rather than beautiful; but there is a lovely squirrel, called a *chipmunk*, small and exceedingly graceful, whose curiosity, prevailing over its timidity, made it a constant and apparently an amused spectator of our proceedings as we jolted along over the roughest of forest and mountain roads. We never came across a snake, though they are said to be abundant. It is disappointing to find comparatively few singing birds; in this respect England is more favoured than America. Every now and then there is a plague of locusts desolating whole districts. Strange to say, if they settle on the line, crushed in myriads under the wheels of the locomotives, they reduce the trains to an absolute standstill, for the rails are so effectually greased that the wheels refuse to bite.

Portland, the most important city of Oregon, was our next resting-place. Here we spent three delightful days, the last of which, as the weather cleared, was glorified by a distant vision of the snow mountains of the Sierra Nevada, recalling the view of the Alps from Berne or the Pyrenees from Pau. The resources of this beautiful place are immense, and are being rapidly developed. As an indication of the abundance of salmon, we were informed that in the agreements which masters make with their servants when board is included, it is expressly stipulated by the latter that they shall not have salmon for dinner more than four days a week! It is interesting to know that stipulations of the same kind are to be found in similar English contracts of the time of Elizabeth. We received much kindness at Portland from Bishop Morris and others, and were sorry to leave, though bound for California, at the end of three days. Embarking at a late hour, we dropped down the river in the night, and spent the next morning at Astoria, gazing out beyond a line of breakers to the Pacific Ocean. It maintained its good character, and justified its name, and we enjoyed a prosperous and rapid voyage of nearly a thousand miles, with a bold coast and mountain outline to the east of us, and many evidences of abounding life in the waters around. We saw many whales spouting. Early on the third morning we reached the Golden Gate, the far-famed mouth of the harbour of San Francisco. There are some spirited lines by Bret Harte on the approach to San Francisco from the sea, which in so few words express so much, that I cannot do better than quote them :—

"Serene, indifferent of Fate,
Thou sittest at the Western Gate ;

" Upon thy heights so lately won
Still slant the banners of the sun ;

" Thou seest the white seas strike their tents
O Warder of two Continents !

" And scornful of the peace that flies
Thy angry winds and sullen skies,

" Thou drawest all things, small or great,
To thee, beside the Western Gate."

San Francisco, the chief city of California, and the commercial metropolis of the Pacific coast, is one of the most remarkable specimens of rapid growth to be met with even in America, the land of gigantic mushrooms. The first house was built in 1835, and by 1848, the year of the discovery of gold in California, the population had increased to a thousand. In 1850 it was twenty-five thousand; and to-day it is said to exceed three hundred thousand. It is the most cosmopolitan city in the world. You may walk through French, Spanish, German, Italian, Mexican, and Chinese colonies one after another; and all the languages of the civilized world may be heard in its busy and crowded streets. The Chinese population alone numbers forty thousand. The quarter occupied by them bears the name of *Chinatown*, and we devoted an evening to it under the guidance of a police constable. The joss-house, or temple, was very similar to one we had visited at Portland, a small chamber richly furnished, and adorned with shrines and idols. Their religious service seems to consist chiefly of prayers and offerings presented with the idea of propitiating gods whom they suspect of malevolence, and regard with contempt, mingled with some measure of superstitious awe. Cups of tea are sometimes placed before their pictures and images, which are repulsively ugly. This, however, is only the popular system, secretly repudiated by the followers of Confucius. Mr. Henry, the author of an interesting book, entitled "The Cross and the Dragon," says, in a chapter on Confucius and Confucianism, "In the matter of speculative religion the mass of Chinese *literati* are atheists, materialists, or at best agnostics; wrapped in the mantle of their literary exclusiveness, they ridicule the worship of idols, even when going through the services as a matter of form; their practice in this respect being on a par with their whole character as professed disciples of the great sage."

We visited some of the haunts of the Chinese below ground, where they herd together in places compared with which a London cellar would be a place of refined comfort. Some were gambling; others were in a state of drowsy intoxication induced by opium-smoking. The Chinese theatre was one of the strangest sights I ever saw. We were conducted through the green-room on to the stage, where we occupied seats close to the performers. And such a performance! The music consisted of the most discordant noises, made by the beating of gongs and other instruments of torture; nor was I able to discover any dignity or grace of action or utterance to compensate for so painful an ordeal. The female parts are always taken by men; and from the floor of the theatre, no less than from the stage, ladies are rigorously excluded. This, our conductor assured us, is a necessary precaution, for their earrings, if they sat with their lords, would certainly be stolen, nor would the thief scruple, in possessing himself of the earring, to appropriate the ear along with it! Accordingly the few ladies who were present—not more than a dozen—sat apart in a box by themselves—"ladies from the ancient and incomprehensible Flowery Land, like fossil bones of an old world sticking out amid the vegetation of the new,"—such is Kingsley's account of a similar company whose presence so startled and disconcerted him when preaching at Savanna Grande.

In strange contrast with all this barbarism was the elegant restaurant, handsomely and tastefully furnished, in which the daintiest meals, consisting largely of delicious bonbons, cakes, and preserved fruits, are served, and with the help of chop-sticks devoured, washed down by cups of fragrant tea. A favourite Chinese dish consists of a bird's nest, but of what kind, and in what way cooked, I was not able to discover.

The Chinese difficulty in America is a very real one. It is only in the towns that they appear to such disadvantage; and even there they are acknowledged to be clever and industrious workmen, and admirable domestic servants. The complaint against them is that they never can be converted into citizens. They come over in thousands, under the direction of Chinese agencies, and on the understanding that they return with their earnings to enrich their native land. Should they die in America, their bones are carefully re-shipped for China. Able to live at a much cheaper rate than others, they are content with very low wages, and this places them at a great advantage in the labour market, and makes them exceedingly unpopular. It remains to be seen whether a solution can be found of the difficulty, without having recourse to repressive legislation which would violate a fundamental principle of the republican constitution. It was a delightful experience, after all that we had seen of them at San Francisco, to visit a Chinese Sunday school at Philadelphia, where we found a band of Christian ladies devoting themselves to the instruction of grateful and intelligent adult pupils. The Americans are great at Sunday schools; and in this way much good is being done among the Chinese in the Eastern States. And here we do well to pause and remind ourselves that, as regards China, we Englishmen have a work of reparation to do. We are largely responsible for the opium traffic that has been, and still is, such a curse to the Chinese. The Anglo-Oriental Society for the suppression of that traffic would seem to be worthy of all support, and, unless its very reasonable demands are granted, we shall be guilty of perpetuating a most grievous national sin. What these demands are I venture to put before you, in the hope that some may be able and willing to come forward and give their support to so good a cause. The Society confines itself to two positive demands:

1. That the British Government in India shall not encourage and promote the opium trade.

2. That all coercion shall be withdrawn from China, and that the government of that country shall be left absolutely free to prohibit the entrance of our opium altogether, or to lay upon it what taxes it pleases.*

From San Francisco we made two expeditions to places of far-famed beauty—Monterey and the Yosemite Valley. Monterey is situated on a beautiful bay, about a hundred miles to the south, and is one of the most interesting of the old Spanish towns on the Pacific coast. It was formerly, under Mexican rule, the seat of government, and a place of some commercial importance; but now it is chiefly interesting as the queen of American watering-places, and the centre of a region of unsurpassed loveliness. I have seldom seen a more exquisite garden than that which surrounds the Hotel del Monte, a grove of stately trees—oaks, pines, and cedars —adorned with sub-tropical plants, and haunted by humming-birds. Delightful was it to take a plunge off the pier-head into the Pacific; and never to be forgotten the coast-drive through pleasant woods and past the huts of the Chinese fishermen, pausing at a rocky headland, flanked by a grove of noble cypresses, round which the waves surged and leapt and loudly murmured with a vehemence worthy of the Atlantic. We spent a lovely Sunday at

* There is, I know, a doubt entertained by some as to the sincerity of the Chinese Government in this matter; but England will not surely excuse herself for promoting an abuse on the ground that China is not in earnest about its suppression.

Monterey, and visited with deep interest the little church of the Franciscan Fathers, an Order whose mission to California began at San Diego in 1769, and at Monterey a year later. In the homely porch we read an account of the Apostolic life and labours of Father Junipero Serra, one of that devoted band of missionaries by whom thousands of the native Indians were gathered into the fold of Christ.* The story of Indian warfare is no doubt one of bloodshed, cruelty, and outrage ; but, if they resented with the ferocity of savages the intrusion of white men who appropriated their hunting grounds and gave them no quarter, let it not be forgotten that they responded generously to the appeal of those who, consecrated by the hands of poverty and pain, spoke to them in the Name of a crucified King, and proclaimed the gospel of peace and goodwill. Not yet, I think, are white men civilized enough to handle savages successfully. And of all savages the red man, perhaps, demands the greatest patience, courtesy, and forbearance. Not yet have we learnt to put

* Let me quote a few characteristic words from a letter by this admirable man. He is imploring the friend to whom he writes to assist in the sending of more missionaries, and concludes with this note of warning :—"Let those who come here come well provided with patience and charity, and let them pass on in good humour for they may become rich : I mean *in troubles :* but where will the labouring ox go where he must not draw the plough? and if he do not draw the plough, how can there be a harvest?" Father Junipero died in 1782, at the age of seventy, "having lived," to quote Father Palou, " in continual activity, occupied in virtuous and holy exercises, and in singular prowesses, all directed to the greater glory of God, and the salvation of souls."

in practice the divine method, though the experience of ages demonstrates the futility of every other, of overcoming evil, not with evil, but with good. The Government of the United States is at length earnestly endeavouring to do tardy justice to the conquered race : but it was distressing to hear again and again from American lips the remark that "a *good* Indian is a *dead* Indian." For my own part I cannot believe that a people whose dark eyes are so wistful and dreamy, whose speech is so musical, and whose language so full of poetry, can be hopelessly degraded, or doomed to extinction.*

But we must tear ourselves away from Monterey and its interesting associations, for the Yosemite Valley awaits us in its romantic seclusion, with its granite cliffs and domes, its stately trees, and its melodious choir of spirit-voices singing the song of waterfalls. On the Feast of Pentecost, 1874, Charles Kingsley preached in the Yosemite, and on the same day, in Westminster Abbey, Dean Stanley alluded to it, and went on to speak of "that wonderful Californian valley, the most beautiful spot on the face of the earth, where the glories of Nature are revealed on the most gigantic scale, a valley to whose trees the cedars of Lebanon are but as the hyssop that groweth out of the wall—where water and forest and sky conjoin to make up, if anywhere on this globe, an earthly paradise."

* In the first chapter of McMaster's history will be found an admirable delineation of the Indian character.

An early train brought us back to San Francisco, and the same afternoon we started for this fairy-land of the West. The valley, which is situated on the western slope of the Sierra Nevada, though little more than a hundred miles from San Francisco, can be reached only by a circuitous route, involving, in addition to a long railway journey, a stage drive of two hundred miles, in and out. It occasionally happens that the stage-coach is "held up," as the expression is, those who do the trick being, like English highwaymen of the last century, armed and masked robbers, who make the customary demand, " Your money or your life." This had occurred at the beginning of the season, and a letter appeared in the *Times* last summer giving an account of the robbery. We were naturally anxious to have a similar adventure, but our hopes were doomed to disappointment. It so happened, however, that the gentlemen of the road were convicted on the very day we started for the Valley, and we had the satisfaction of announcing the welcome tidings all along the road. The presence of mind of one lady was much commended, who, while she was urgently beseeching her husband to surrender his purse rather than sacrifice his life, adroitly concealed a bundle of dollar-notes in the recesses of a sandwich!

We entered the Yosemite Valley by Inspiration Point, thus obtaining a magnificent view of its green and grey loveliness from the high ground. It is only about twelve miles in length, and very narrow. "The principal features of the Yosemite," to quote Professor Whitney, State geologist of California, "and those by which it is distinguished from all other known valleys are—(1) The near approach to verticality of its walls; (2) Their great height, not only absolutely, but as compared with the width of the valley itself; and (3) the very small amount of *débris* at the base of these gigantic cliffs." The valley is singularly rich in waterfalls, two of the loveliest of which bear the poetical names of the Bridal Veil and the Virgin's Tears. The loftiest is the Yosemite Fall, which measures in all 2600 feet, including first a vertical leap of 1500 feet, and then, after a series of cascades, a final plunge of 400 feet to the base of the precipice. This, however, must be seen in the spring; after the summer heats it dwindles and almost disappears. The Nevada Fall at the head of the valley, to which we climbed on horseback, is at all seasons full, and remarkably beautiful, encircled by noble cliffs. But I despair of giving any idea of the majesty of the whole scene, in harmonious combination with every form of delicate beauty. The trees, the shrubs, the flowers —all are exquisite. In such an enchanted land you would expect to find the native Indians graceful and gracious,—children of the west wind, like Longfellow's Hiawatha; bold as the lion, swift as the deer, like the last of the Mohicans; but alas! it is not so. The red men of the Yosemite are among the most degraded of their race; they are called

Digger Indians, and support themselves on a diet of roots and snails.

The day of our departure was a specially enjoyable one. We were in the saddle before the sun was up, and, mounting by a steep trail to Glazier Point, reached, after an ascent of two hours, a glorious forest, through which a rapid ride of fifteen miles brought us to the stage road in time to catch the returning coach. In the afternoon we visited the Mariposa grove of big trees, Wellingtonias, intermingled with black sugar pines and Douglas spruce. There are some hundreds of these venerable giants, whose age is to be reckoned, not by hundreds but by thousands of years. Through one a hole has been cut making an archway through which we drove the coach and four horses. Into another, which is hollow and prostrate, three horsemen can ride abreast. The largest bears the not very appropriate name of the Grizzly Giant. It is thirty-one feet in diameter, ninety-four in circumference; the first branch is nearly two hundred feet from the ground, and is six feet in diameter. But no measurements can give any idea of the towering majesty of these trees. No leopard or tiger skin is more exquisitely marked than the bark of their dappled trunks. The cone is a splendid thing; I longed to bring one home; but it would have required a roomy hat-box for its accommodation. What must the roots be like upholding such strength, and at how great a distance from the crown of green foliage! Truly it is a place of solemn and worshipful beauty, a sanctuary not less glorious than Carmel and Lebanon, "a joy for many generations."

Before leaving San Francisco we paid a visit to Cliff House, a place of favourite resort, from which a beautiful view is obtained of the rocky coast on each side of the Golden Gate. One of the outstanding rocks was simply swarming with sea-lions, whose ceaseless and riotous barking was even more discordant than the gongs of the Chinese theatre. On Michaelmas Day, our last day at San Francisco, we attended an early service at the church of S. Francis, who seems to be the patron-saint of California. In the poem by Bret Harte already quoted, this connection is referred to in some striking lines in which he calls upon the sea-fog to shroud the guilty city :—

"Drop down, O fleecy Fog! and hide
Her sceptic sneer, and all her pride.

"Wrap her, O Fog, in gown and hood
Of her Franciscan Brotherhood.

"Hide me her faults, her sin and blame;
With thy grey mantle cloak her shame.

"So shall she, cowlèd, sit and pray
Till morning bears her sins away.

"Then rise, O fleecy Fog! and raise
The glory of her coming days."

The next day we started for Los Angeles, a journey of nearly five hundred miles due south. It it a lovely place, situated upon the slope of the

Sierra Santa Monica, and girdled with orange groves and vineyards. The Spaniards founded it in 1781, and it had acquired, by the time of the American conquest, some importance. One delightful drive we had through a paradise of fruit trees, by the Sierra Madre Villa to San Gabrielle, in the course of which an unknown benefactor, at whose house we paused for the sake of the view, literally filled the carriage with delicious grapes. At Los Angeles we touched our farthest point. Pursuing our journey we now struck inland, and traversing Arizona, a semi-tropical region, rich in precious metals, where we encountered a party of the United States army in pursuit of Indians on the war-trail, we reached, after two days and nights in the cars, Santa Fé, the capital of New Mexico, and the oldest city in America.

Santa Fé had been described to us as "a sleepy old Mexican city." An old Mexican city it certainly is, but we found it anything but sleepy. The houses, most of them built of mud, or "adobe," as it is called, are flat-roofed, giving the place an oriental and picturesque appearance. We were fortunate enough to arrive on the eve of a great *festa*, and every effort was being made to keep it with all befitting solemnity in honour of the sweet poet-peasant saint of Assisi, whom Mexicans, as well as Indians, have such cause to love and venerate. The cathedral was crowded for Vespers at six o'clock, and the setting sun sent a flood of golden glory through the open western doors, making the scene a singularly impressive one. As in Spanish churches, there were no seats; the women squatted, the men stood; all had the appearance of being devout worshippers. The venerable Archbishop Lamy, who for many years has been a father to the Indians of that district, was the officiating minister at Benediction. The service was followed by an illumination; bonfires were lighted in front of the great church, the village band paraded the streets, and guns were fired which ceased only for a brief interval, renewing their summons to church at five o'clock on the following (Sunday) morning. We assisted at the High Mass, which occupied three hours, some hundreds of men, apparently members of a confraternity, making their communion. The behaviour of the whole vast congregation was most edifying, and it was altogether a strikingly impressive and touching solemnity. We visited the old palace which for centuries was the seat of government, and the ancient church of San Miguel, an interesting little sanctuary, said to be the oldest in America. Next day we somewhat reluctantly continued our journey, and on the following day regained Colorado Springs.

Here we lingered for a delightful week, riding or driving daily, exploring the parks and canyons of one of the most beautiful mountain regions that the world contains. Colorado has been called "a symphony in red and yellow," and these are the predominant colours, but the expression is inadequate, for it gives no hint of the ever-shifting blue shadows that haunt the plains, and the light greenery of the delicate foliage. Colorado Springs is situated on the eastern slope of the Rocky Mountains, seventy miles south of Denver, at a height of 6000 feet. A gently undulating plain slopes away to the east for some hundreds of miles, occasionally broken by wooded bluffs, capital ground for a gallop. I shall never forget a ride through the Garden of the Gods to Glen Eyrie, the romantic home of General Palmer, which it was my good fortune to take in the second week of October. The trees were gathering their loveliest autumn tints, and the blood-red rocks, some of them reaching a height of 350 feet, stood up on all sides in every kind of fantastic shape, under the shadow of the purple mountains. The little mountain valley is indeed an enchanted spot, a sacred enclosure, well fitted by nature to enshrine a vision of the Holy Grail. We made the ascent of Pike's Peak, which from Manitou is an easy expedition of about ten hours, and you can ride the whole way. Up to timber-line, about 10,000 feet, it is exceedingly beautiful, but the summit itself, though the views of course are extensive, is disappointing, consisting of some fifty acres of rocks and snow, without a peak of any kind. It reminded me of the summit of Ben Nevis. The following verses were suggested by the ascent of this famous mountain, founded on the verse with which the first lesson of the preceding evening began:—" In the last days it shall come to pass that the mountain of the House of the Lord shall be established in the top of the mountains, and it shall be exalted above the hills; and people shall flow unto it."

> God's House a lofty mountain is,
>   A holy, happy Home, wherein
> His sons and daughters taste the bliss
>   Of life that knows no sin.
>
> Established is this citadel,
>   The sanctuary of truth and grace;
> Gathered therein Love's vassals dwell,
>   Oh, 'tis a wealthy place!
>
> God's handiwork! exalted high,
>   Of Love's own loveliness fulfilled;
> Mighty is He to beautify
>   What He alone can build.
>
> God's mountain-top! the nations flow
>   Through gates that ever open stand;
> Upward is ever homeward; so
>   Gain we our Fatherland.
>
> Here in this beauty-haunted spot,
>   Discerning "shadows of the True,"
> I pluck this one forget-me-not,
>   And give it, friend, to you.

To traverse any great mountain range, or to make the acquaintance of any lofty peak, is a privilege my sense of which is in large measure due to the teaching of Ruskin; and the truth of his words is realized in the Rocky Mountains not less than among his favourite Alps. In an eloquent chapter of *Modern Painters*, after insisting on the three great uses of mountains—(1) "to give motion to water," (2) "to maintain a constant change in the currents and nature of the air," and (3) "to cause perpetual change in the soils of the earth," he concludes thus : " These desolate and threatening ranges of dark mountains, which in nearly all ages of the world men have looked upon with aversion or with terror, and have shrunk back from as if they were haunted by perpetual images of death, are in reality sources of life and happiness far fuller and more beneficent than all the bright fruitfulness of the plain. The valleys only feed; the mountains feed and guard and strengthen us. We take our idea of fearfulness and sublimity alternately from the mountain and the sea; but we associate them unjustly. The sea-wave, with all its beneficence, is yet devouring and terrible; but the silent wave of the blue mountain is lifted towards heaven in a stillness of perpetual mercy; and the one surge unfathomable in its darkness, the other unshaken in its faithfulness, for ever bear the seal of their appointed symbolism—

"Thy righteousness is like the great mountains;
Thy judgments are a great deep."

Colorado is a famous country for ranches, and I was sorry we did not see more of the cattle-men and cow-boys. The latter gallop about all day with swinging arms, a loose rein, a cruel spur, and a loaded whip. They are somewhat reckless, not to say lawless, in their methods and habits of life; in illustration whereof let me tell you a story which I had on good authority. Determined to have some fun out of an unhappy Frenchman, whose high-heeled Parisian boots excited their curiosity, they invited him to spend the evening with them. Whereupon, forming in a ring round their guest, they requested him to dance for their diversion, a demand which they proceeded to enforce by taking pistol-shots at his heels. So persuasively urged, he was constrained to caper about with surprising agility, nor was he permitted to slacken without being promptly reminded by a renewal of the cow-boys' music that the entertainment must proceed.

Hard work was it bidding farewell to beautiful Colorado Springs, and all the friends there who had been so kind to me and mine; but time was running short, and with so much still to be seen on the eastern coast we could not prolong our stay. A journey of two thousand miles brought us to Washington, stopping for a day only at St. Louis, a city of great commercial importance from its position on the Mississippi, and in the centre of the great basin of the continent, but possessing no beauty. The buildings are singularly poor; the river, though broad enough, is muddy and sluggish. A visit to some exquisite gardens five miles out of town, said to be the best in the whole country, amply repaid us for the delay; but it was exhilarating to find ourselves at length at Washington, in very different and much more beautiful quarters. Washington is, of those we saw, the one really beautiful city on the eastern side of the continent, and every year adds to its charms. The absence of business, except that which connects itself with politics and government offices, is no doubt in a large measure the cause of this. Since 1800 it has been the political centre and capital of the United States. We went at once to the Capitol, and devoted a morning to its investigation. It is, both for beauty and interest, pre-eminent among the buildings of the western continent, and Americans may well be pardoned if they rank it among the great buildings of the world. It was founded by Washington himself in 1794, and has been growing ever since, though still far from completion. It contains the Council-chambers of the Senators and Representatives, the Supreme Court of Justice, the Congress Library, and a number of handsome rooms, including a vast Rotunda, the centre of the building, surmounted by a lofty dome, and a National Statuary Hall, adorned with statues and busts, of small artistic merit, but great historical interest, representing American statesmen, among them Washington, Hamilton, Jefferson, and Lincoln. The wings of the building are of white marble, perfect in design, and of a most beautiful complexion. In a land so destitute of outward symbols of the Faith, it was a pleasant surprise to find in a building so central and so supreme, pictures representing the two great sacramental ministries of cleansing and feeding. The baptism of an Indian maiden is one of the subjects that adorn the Rotunda, and in the

Chamber of Representatives the altar of the Eucharist is depicted, reared on the Californian coast, and surrounded by worshipping peasants. When the central part of the building, which at present consists of free-stone painted, is reconstructed and made to correspond with the marble wings, one would gladly see substituted for the figure of Liberty at the summit of the dome, an image of the world's Liberator, with the motto subscribed in characters of light, "Stand fast therefore in the liberty wherewith Christ hath made us free."

The river expedition to Mount Vernon is one that no visitor to Washington should omit to make. Mount Vernon was George Washington's patrimonial estate; here his last days were spent; here he died, and here is his tomb. It occupies a beautiful position on the Virginia side of the Potomac, fifteen miles below the city. It is now the property of the nation, and is carefully preserved in the state in which it was when occupied by the hero of American history—a homely, comfortable, old-fashioned house, with a broad verandah and a sloping lawn above the river. There are several interesting relics—among others, the key of the Bastille, presented by the remarkable Frenchman who did so much for American independence, La Fayette.

A letter of introduction with which we were furnished secured us a welcome at the White House, and a few minutes' conversation with President

Cleveland. It was a pleasure to grasp the hand of a man who, in the midst of the corruption that discredits political life in the United States, not only bears an unblemished reputation, but also, at the risk of forfeiting popularity and alienating many members of his own party, is courageous enough to introduce and press forward much-needed reforms. Is it too much to hope that all patriotic Americans, whether Democrats or Republicans, will rally round him in the prosecution of the difficult task to which he has set his hand? I am inclined to think, though the suspicion may be an erroneous one, that the democratic fervour and enthusiasm, which in Europe has found its creed in the concise and comprehensive formula, " Liberty, Equality, Fraternity," and which in such a man as Mazzini reaches the height and possesses the force of a spiritual conviction, is little known in America. Liberty no doubt is held in honour, but Fraternity and Equality can hardly be said to be governing principles in the social and political life of the country. It is one more evidence, if that were needed, of the inadequacy of a humanitarian system, when the theological significance of the symbols employed is disallowed, and Liberty, Equality, and Fraternity are not balanced and supplemented, and so really enforced and safeguarded, by a recognition of the truths that are represented by the words, no less beautiful and venerable—Obedience, Subordination, Fatherhood.

With reference to the religious condition of the

country, I hesitate to say even a word. Evening shadows still haunt the Garden of the Tree of Life, and its fruits are hidden. In America, no less than in Europe, the wounds of the Church gape and bleed, and the confusion of Babel-voices drowns the harmony of the Spiritual City. But here, as elsewhere, error bears witness to truth, and the vitality of a system or a sect is to be found, not in the perversion of a truth, but in its survival in spite of perversion. The Shakers, for example, all celibates living in community, by the serenity and simplicity of their industrious and self-denying lives, bear a testimony to the reality of the life of *Counsels* that is undeniable. Perhaps it is for the rise of a great monastic legislator and reformer with the wisdom of a S. Benedict, the devotion of a S. Francis, and the genius of a S. Thomas Aquinas, that we may most reasonably look, taught by the past history of the Church, as God's instrument to awaken the conscience and convince the understanding of this great, enterprising, and intelligent people.

It was at Baltimore, our next halting-place and the principal city of Maryland, that we saw and heard most of the coloured people. They frequent in great numbers S. Mary's, a daughter-church of Mount Calvary, by whose clergy we were kindly welcomed. Thoroughly acquainted with all the conditions of the negro-problem, these devoted priests work on undiscouraged, looking for fruit in the future rather than the present, and pleading for patience and forbearance in dealing with a race that has only just emerged from slavery. There are those who say that the negro will ever be in the future what he has been in the past—a liar, a thief, and a profligate; but they whose knowledge is the outcome of loving and self-sacrificing service tell a very different tale. The evil can by the grace of God be eradicated. Children the negroes are, no doubt, and children in point of intelligence they will probably remain for many years to come; but that is a condition that carries with it no disability in the spiritual kingdom whose mysteries are revealed to babes. The awakened conscience of the nation has emancipated them; they have been, perhaps prematurely, enfranchised and entrusted with all the rights and duties of citizenship; it remains to educate and develop them, not by patronage or indulgence, but by giving them a fair field, with a generous recognition of their good points, and a sustained and serious endeavour to obliterate the line of social separation. Under such treatment who can doubt that this long-afflicted and much-enduring African race will find at length its true position, and that a useful and honourable one, in this great Western continent, where, thank God, there is room enough for all? There is at Baltimore a branch of the All Saints' Sisterhood, and the Sisters have been enterprising enough to undertake the training of several coloured women for community-life, an attempt which already bids fair to prove successful.

It was a joy to see three of these gentle daughters of Africa in the religious habit.

From Baltimore we went to Philadelphia, spending a night on the way pleasantly with friends among the Quakers of Germantown, a delightful suburb of a delightful city. Philadelphia, the capital of Pennsylvania, and the largest city as to area in the United States, lies on the west bank of the Delaware river, ninety miles from the Atlantic. To William Penn, the Quaker, a man of good birth, large fortune, high character, and unquestionable capacity, Pennsylvania, a large, beautiful, and fruitful estate, was granted in satisfaction of a debt by Charles II. By him Philadelphia was founded, and great homage is rendered to him there as to a canonized saint and patron. A colossal image of him is about to be erected on the lofty summit of the new municipal buildings, which, like most public buildings in America, are costly and pretentious, but singularly destitute of picturesque charm and artistic beauty. Our time in Philadelphia was chiefly devoted to the examination of public institutions. We visited schools, hospitals, museums, libraries, reformatories, prisons. All seemed to be admirable, and not, to any very marked extent, unlike similar institutions in England. In elementary schools we have probably something to learn from America, though the system of free education is, I venture to think, of questionable advantage; but the absence of anything at all corresponding to our great public schools will be regarded by most Englishmen as a serious defect. The extreme comfort of prison-life surprised us not a little. We found in the cells of convicted criminals daily papers, pictures, musical instruments, and tobacco! Nothing could more clearly demonstrate the non-existence in America of a large, miserable, poverty-stricken class like that which chiefly recruits the criminal population in all European cities. In England to furnish a prison cell with such comforts would be to put a premium on crime. A school for Indian girls, where we found a hundred happy little brown-faced maidens, and heard not only their singing, but their laughter, was, after what we had seen on the Indian reservations of the West, a specially delightful sight. Our Sunday at Philadelphia we spent chiefly at S. Clement's, the church of the Evangelist Fathers, over which Father Maturin presides.

Continuing our journey, regaled all the way by a perfect feast of colour, the autumn tints being now in their full glory, we reached Staten Island, which is virtually a beautiful suburb of New York, and spent three days very pleasantly at S. Mary's Rectory, paying daily visits to the great city. It has been said that, if Venice was the city of the Doges, New York is the city of the *dodges*. Certainly the genius of Americans for mechanical inventions and appliances is here seen to great advantage. "Shadows of the coming race" fall fast on every side, and one cannot but share the apprehensions so forcibly expressed by George Eliot in the article which bears that title in "Theophrastus Such." "When one considers," she says, "the perfunctory way in which some of the most exalted tasks are already executed by those who are understood to be educated for them, there rises a fearful vision of the human race evolving machinery which will by-and-by throw itself fatally out of work. When in the Bank of England I see a wondrously delicate machine for testing sovereigns, a shrewd, implacable little steel Rhadamanthus that, once the keys are delivered up to it, lifts and balances each in turn for the fraction of an instant, finds it wanting or sufficient, and dismisses it to right or left with rigorous justice; when I am told of micrometers and thermopiles and tasimeters which deal physically with the invisible, the impalpable and the unimaginable; of cunning wires and wheels and pointing needles which will register your and my quickness so as to exclude flattering opinion; of a machine for drawing the right conclusion, which will doubtless by-and-by be improved into an automaton for finding true premises; of a microphone which detects the cadences of the fly's foot on the ceiling, and may be expected presently to discriminate the noises of our various follies as they soliloquize or converse in our brains—my mind seeming too small for these things, I get a little out of it, like an unfortunate savage too suddenly brought face to face with civilization, and I exclaim, Am I already in the shadow of the coming race? and will the creatures who are to transcend and finally supersede us be steely organisms, giving out the effluvia of the laboratory, and performing with infallible exactness more than everything that we have performed with a slovenly approximativeness and self-defeating inaccuracy?"

The development and multiplication of machinery is a doubtful gain. Mr. Pidgeon, the author of "Old World Questions and New World Answers," tells a story of an ingenious American who invented a machine for extracting the bones of a certain fish. By a skilfully contrived double action the bones were discarded, and the fish presented to the mouth; but one day in a moment of emotion or forgetfulness the inventor put the wrong end of his machine to his mouth, and all the bones went down his throat; whereupon he miserably perished, and his secret perished with him!

But let us not forget that it is in America itself that a warning voice has been raised. "Beauty," says Emerson, "must come back to the useful arts, and the distinction between the fine and the useful arts be forgotten. If history were truly told, if life were nobly spent, it would be no longer easy or possible to distinguish the one from the other. In nature all is useful, all is beautiful. It is therefore beautiful, because it is alive, moving, reproductive; it is therefore useful, because it is symmetrical and fair." So the sage of Concord insists; and again:

"Is not the selfish and even cruel aspect which belongs to our great mechanical works—to mills, railways, and machinery—the effect of the mercenary impulses which these works obey? When its errands are noble and adequate, a steamboat bridging the Atlantic between Old and New England, and arriving at its ports with the punctuality of a planet, is a step of man into harmony with nature. . . . When science is learned in love, and its powers are wielded by love, they will appear the supplements and continuations of the material creation."

It cannot be denied that American ingenuity and industry have done much in this department for which we may well be thankful. For example, there is a factory at Waterbury, in Massachusetts, which turns out an admirable time-keeper, known as "the Waterbury watch," at the rate of six hundred a day, or one per minute. The price of this watch is only two dollars forty-three cents, or rather less than ten shillings. Mr. Pidgeon devotes an interesting chapter to "Clockland," which gives a delightful impression of the activity, enterprise, cleanliness, and cheerfulness of the factories which abound in New England.

I have been trying to register impressions. It will be said, perhaps, that they are all favourable. No, not all; though the pleasant ones would rightly take precedence, even if they did not far outnumber the others. To those familiar with the sanctuaries of Europe, it must be admitted that America has

E

the outward aspect of an unchristened country. There are no wayside, or churchyard crosses, no holy wells, no shady cloisters; up the mountain-paths climb no stations of the cross leading to rustic chapel or calvary; in the shadow of church porches no enniched Madonna lifts enthroned upon her bosom the Holy Child; from the lowly belfries of village and hamlet no bells with their melodious chimes "make Catholic the trembling air." The very churches themselves, well carpeted and cushioned as they are, look little like places of worship. To all of which two answers may be made by Christian lips:—(1) It may be said, This is a new country, and has had as yet no time to embellish itself with those outward adornments which the piety of many generations has transmitted to us the children of the Old World. This, however, would appear to be an unsatisfactory explanation in the presence of such abounding luxury, and in a country where all the mechanical appliances that make life comfortable, are found in a degree of excellence unsurpassed, perhaps unequalled, in any European land. (2) Or again, it may be argued, Christianity is a living faith, inspired by the spirit of progress, and of necessity new forms and methods of expression supersede the old. Most true; but where may the new expressions be found? As long as human nature remains essentially unchanged, in spite of, or rather because of, unceasing advance and development, that which is inwardly realized will surely find some means of outward expression. The Church of Christ is a pilgrim-queen who cannot but leave her footprint on every path by which she journeys homeward. It is for these footprints that we may reasonably look, and the absence of which may not unreasonably cause distress. Let us, however, charitably hope that it is only because our eyes are dim that we discern them not.

But it is not only the absence of the lovely and familiar symbols of things unseen that one remarks and regrets. There are everywhere ugly signs of a huckstering, commercial spirit, vulgar and mendacious, against which it cannot but be a kindness to protest. I was already familiar with the new American version of the old couplet:—

"Early to bed and early to rise,
Is no good unless you advertise."

But nothing that I had heard had prepared me for the detestable vulgarity of the whole advertising system. The trees that fringe Niagara, the crimson rocks of the Colorado canyons, the stately giants of the Californian groves—all are disfigured by these abominable advertisements. The newspapers, already sufficiently repulsive, are of course full of them.

But we must suspend these reflections and pursue our journey. It was not without emotion that we set foot in Boston at an early hour on the Vigil of All Saints. *The Pilgrim*, most magnificent of floating palaces, had brought us by night from New

York, and slowly and sadly did the day break as we landed at Fall River, and gazed for the first time on a New England landscape. The capital of Massachusetts, though much of the old city has been destroyed by fire, will ever be interesting as the first theatre of that great struggle, which ended so fortunately for all concerned in the discomfiture of England, and made of the disunited colonies the United States. Strangely, indeed, has Boston changed since the days of the first settlers, although it is a change for which the student of history is not unprepared. The Pilgrim Fathers were, no doubt, like the founders of the Spanish Inquisition, stern, resolute, courageous, conscientious and devoted men; but the one system, no less than the other, has proved a disastrous failure. Their theology reproduced some of the worst features of the later scholasticism, their methods were harsh and tyrannical, and their laws frequently both childish and cruel. Mothers, for example, were forbidden to kiss their children on the Sabbath; and absence from the conventicle (where the sermon often lasted for three hours) was treated as a crime, and punished on a second offence by public exposure in the stocks. The system, in short, established by men who left England to protest against the tyranny of kings and priests, was itself a spiritual tyranny far more oppressive than that from which they had fled. The same harsh and relentless spirit discovered itself in other relations, and New England has been too truly called "the slaughter-house of the Indians." The inevitable reaction has followed; rigour has given place to laxity;* and a fierce and narrow Calvinism has been superseded by a religion of culture and refinement, which, with all its charm, is sadly wanting in spiritual power to purify and regenerate, and in great danger of contemplating every creed only to reject them all.

Our last afternoon was devoted to Cambridge, where, under the guidance of Professor James, the brother of the well-known novelist, from whom we received great kindness, we visited Harvard University. Though modern in comparison with our own ancient universities, it is no mushroom, having been founded in 1638 by an English clergyman, whose name it bears. The buildings are numerous and handsome. Longfellow's house was also pointed out to us, and the old tree under which Washington unfurled the standard of rebellion. Among eminent Bostonians with whom it was our privilege to become acquainted, it is a special pleasure to record two names—Oliver Wendell Holmes and Phillips Brooks. The veteran poet, author of "The Autocrat of the Breakfast Table," is as pleasant and amusing as his books. From his study-window he showed us a fine view of the city, pointing out the Bunker's Hill Monument, which, as he gracefully remarked, mindful of our nationality, commemorates,

---

* Miss Martineau, who had ample means of judging, speaks sadly of the immorality of New England.

unlike most other monuments, *a defeat*. The great preacher, so well-known in England, we were fortunate enough to hear twice in his own church, and with a growing sense of an intellectual, moral, and spiritual force, the glad recognition of which by all classes and parties at Boston is a significant fact. The cultivated Unitarianism of Boston is doomed. It was the natural and inevitable reaction from the Puritanism of the early settlers, and their Calvinistic misrepresentation of God, and virtual denial of His Unity. Among the most thoughtful and devout of those who have been influenced by this reaction, a pantheistic tendency, as in the case of Emerson, may already be detected, which renders an unconscious homage to the Christian conception of an Eternal Generation and an Eternal Procession in God, whereby He is ever giving and spending Himself under the constraint of Love—a Divine Activity of which Creation is the visible sacrament, and Humanity the latest-born child. Matthew Arnold is surely right in attributing to Emerson the distinction of being, among men of the New World, a master spiritual influence; and this, if I read his mental history aright, is the upward path trod by the feet of that singularly gifted and gracious man. I was much occupied with his life and writings during my visit to America, and the following verses, which will certainly please neither his worshippers nor his detractors, are a slight tribute of affection to his memory :—

> Not with the seers his niche, nor where
> Wisdom enshrined uplifts her torch ;
> But in the balmy, sunlit air
> Of Truth's wide open temple-porch.
>
> Hers was his harp ; his heart was hers ;
> And hence his mission cannot fail,
> Interpreting the characters
> Inwoven on the outer veil.
>
> 'Twas hidden manna that he sought,
> His pilgrimage was one ascent ;
> With mystery and meaning fraught
> To him was Nature's sacrament.
>
> May men to larger stature grow,
> May greener laurels still be won ;
> Yet flowers ever fresh shall blow
> Upon the grave of Emerson.

Our stay at Boston was all too short. It is the metropolis of learning and refinement, and we found it no less hospitable than cultivated. We were kindly welcomed among others by the Evangelist Fathers, and spent a Sunday with them very happily. Breaking the return journey to New York, half a day was all that we were able to devote to Newport, the most celebrated and popular of American watering-places. A century ago it was a place of commercial importance, but now it is the headquarters of pleasure and fashion. A walk which we took in the fading light of an autumn afternoon, across green lawns sloping down to the cliffs, to the music of whispering waves, was one that will not be forgotten ; nor the kindness of friends whose hospitable welcome made the strange and lovely place seem almost homelike.

To the question often asked—Are American ladies as beautiful as English? an Englishman can of course give only one answer; but that a high order of beauty belongs to American ladies, and a beauty that has its own very special and fascinating charm, I am prepared to maintain against all comers. On this subject I cannot do better than quote some lines from "A Letter from Newport," a poem by Mr. Myers, in which, with his accustomed felicity, he indicates most successfully wherein that charm lies :—

> "Through English eyes more calmly soft
>   Looks from grey deeps the appealing charm;
> Reddens on English cheeks more oft
>   The rose of innocent alarm:
> Our old-world heart more gravely feels,
>   Has learnt more force, more self-control;
> For us through sterner music peals
>   The full accord of soul and soul.
>
> "But, ah, the life, the smile untaught,
>   The floating presence, feathery-fair!
> The eyes and aspect that have caught
>   The brilliance of Columbian air!
> No oriole through the forest flits
>   More sheeny-plumed, more gay and free;
> On no nymph's marble forehead sits
>   Proudlier a glad virginity."

And yet it must, I fear, be admitted that America is not the land of romance.* The prevailing money-

* Hawthorne acknowledges that America is not the country

making spirit is sadly fatal to high ideals, fatal in the long run to all true nobility of life. American marriages are, it is to be feared, too often a matter of speculation, if not of bargain. The cause of Woman's Rights is of all causes the most sacred, but it may well be questioned whether the American methods of advocating it are the best. Woman casts away her sceptre, and descends from her throne, when she prides herself on being man's competitor and antagonist rather than his inspirer and helpmeet. Beauty, when she ceases to be bashful, discrowns herself, and forfeits no little of the homage that is her due. The conditions of life in America are such that all who are submitted to them are in danger of developing a calculating shrewdness and a superficial smartness inconsistent with the deep convictions and lofty aspirations out of which a life rightly and worthily inspired is fashioned. And an uninspired life—an unimpassioned life—is a treason against Love. The corruptions and desecrations of our Old World civilization are indeed patent and scandalous. With shame and sorrow we can but confess and deplore them. All the more on that account are we conscious of disappointment and regret, if, by all that we see and hear, the conclusion is forced upon for the scene of a romance, on the score that it is too prosperous, too happy, too free "from any picturesque and gloomy wrong!"— a conclusion in which any one, not an American, will, I think, hesitate to acquiesce.

us against our will that things are little, if at all, better in the rising civilization of the West.

One of our last days at New York was shadowed by a sorrow. The flags were flying half-mast high, and the evening papers told us the reason, announcing the sudden death of one of the most distinguished heroes of the war—General McClellan. He was Commander-in-Chief of the United States army before Grant, and his name is associated with the stubborn resistance offered to the Confederate forces when, in the early stages of the desperate struggle, they were flushed with success, and the position of affairs was most critical.* For two or three pleasant days in Colorado and Utah he and his family had been our travelling companions, and, on parting at Salt Lake City, we had gladly accepted a kind invitation to visit them at Orange, on our return to the eastern coast—an engagement the fulfilment of which we were anticipating with much pleasure when these sad tidings arrived. On our landing we had found New York in mourning for Grant, and again the shadow of death fell across our path as we turned our faces homeward.

We saw Mary Anderson at New York. Was it a vain fancy that discerned in the old myth of Pygmalion and Galatea, interpreted by the delicate sensibility and quick artistic intelligence of one of

* An able article by General McClellan on "The Peninsular Campaign," will be found in the *Century Magazine* of May, 1885.

the most accomplished of American ladies, a story not without significance in connection with the past, present, and future of America? Is man in danger more there than elsewhere of being dazzled by the splendour of his own achievements? and is a civilization full of beauty born out of due time, suddenly liberated, and intoxicated with the rapture and exuberance of new life, destined to be as suddenly disillusioned, as the unsuspected depths and currents of passion by which it is swayed and moulded reveal themselves, with the complications, entanglements, and disasters that wait upon their collision? The grand lesson is at least suggested, which is applicable under all conditions to all nations as to all individuals, that self-sacrificing love is the remedy by which alone all wrongs are righted. But the return to cold marble death as the outcome of such heroism is the pagan conception of an incomplete and inadequate redemption, falsified for ever by the gospel of the Resurrection. And yet to no other conclusion can man point who looks to himself for the deliverance that can come only from above. Have we not here the warning that America and, indeed, all modern material civilization needs, and which it must lay to heart, if its last state of creedless, godless, self-glorifying atheism is not to be worse than its first? The question will present itself—What is the destiny of this great nation? what shall emerge from the womb of the Future when the New World shall have grown old,—when America is as crowded as

Europe? Will it bind or break? stand or fall? Will the last act of the great drama of human history be enacted there, or, like the middle act, in Europe, or, like the first, in the cradle-lands of the East? and will the conclusion be a catastrophe or a victorious consummation? Ah! what shall be disclosed by the bright light of the last and grandest Epiphany; when the morning stars find voice for an evening hymn; and, heralding another sunrise, Gabriel again blows his trumpet in the morning—the new morning of a heavenly day? These are questions that impose silence; but not, for Christians at least, the silence of despair; we look for new heavens and a new earth, wherein shall dwell Righteousness.

Before embarking we dined with Mr. Cyrus Field, to whom belongs the distinction of having laid the first Atlantic cable; and my last hour in America was spent at the bedside of a gentle sufferer, who for years has been set apart, in the cloister of a sick chamber, for a ministry of gracious influence by which many have been blest. Above her bed hung a print of Raphael's Transfiguration, to which she drew my attention. It was the fitting conclusion. Our eyes had looked upon many lovely visions in the New World, but *there* was the crowning vision, the vision that alone is adequate, that alone is permanent, by which all others must be interpreted, and apart from which they are meaningless. And the painter who represents on one canvas the glory that crowned the mountain and the trouble and anguish at its foot, helps us to learn the lesson that light quenches darkness, good conquers evil, joy survives sorrow; for the glory that seemed to fade away on the summit reappears at the foot of the mount in a work of healing and deliverance, and from the quivering lips of the grateful father, gladdened by the recovery of his afflicted child, there comes an echo of that heavenly Voice heard on the mountain-top, "This is my beloved son, in whom I am well pleased." Here was a vision and a lesson to encourage one who was turning his face from the sunshine, the beauty and the wonder of the Western Continent to London work, and the anxieties and desolations of heart that are inseparable from it. How, indeed, could life under any aspect, under any conditions, be faced, if it were not that the Transfigured Christ lives with those words upon His lips, "Behold, I make all things new."

The following verses, with which I will conclude, were written in California, but finished on the Atlantic, when we were steering for England and for home. It was the last Sunday afternoon, and we were nearing the coast of Ireland; the ship was gallantly plunging forward in the face of a head-wind; the movement of the encircling waters was grand, almost rhythmic; like living creatures the waves seemed to be treading a stately measure, with deliberate rise and fall, curve and bend, advance and retreat; the brooding gleam of a wintry sunset was faintly gilding the western horizon, when to my astonished eyes a sign appeared, like that which once gladdened the home-sick heart of a sleeping wayfarer at Bethel—a glory-ladder planted its foot upon the moving waters, and mounted upwards to the sky, like a golden stair connecting heaven and earth for the passage of angels' feet. It was, I thought, a happy omen, indicating the aim and direction of man's long life-voyage from the salt waters to the sweet.

THE NEW WORLD.

A new world did Columbus find?
  Ah! 'tis not so *that* world is found;
God's golden harvest-sheaves who bind
  Are tillers of another ground.

No new world like the old we need;
  One thing suffices—one alone,
A garnered world-harvest from seed
  The wounded Hands of Christ have sown.

No earthly Paradise avails,
  No Eldorado in the West;
The Spirit's Breath must fill their sails
  Who seek the Highlands of the Blest.

By stripes is healing wrought, and stars
  Point ever to a central Sun;
He flies the conquering flag, Whose scars,
  Transfigured, speak of Victory won.

O Royal Heart, Thy Kingdom come!
All else may change; all else may go:
Not eastward, westward, is our Home,
But *onward, upward :*—even so!

One Sign alone is love-designed,
God's Evergreen, the Eternal Rood;
Happy the home-seekers who find
Its meaning plain—*a world renewed!*

THE END.

www.ingramcontent.com/pod-product-compliance
Lightning Source LLC
Chambersburg PA
CBHW031609110426
42742CB00037B/1464